Pay Per Click Marketing:

Best practice strategies to win new customers using Google AdWords and PPC

Phil Robinson • Lindsey Annison
Foreword by Dave Chaffey

ClickThrough Marketing

3

the search conversion experts

Pay Per Click Marketing: Best practice strategies to win new customers using Google AdWords and PPC, 1st Edition

Published by
ClickThrough Marketing,
Charter House, Sandford Street, Lichfield, WS13 6QA
www.clickthrough-marketing.com

ISBN 978-1-907603-02-0

For information on all ClickThrough Marketing publications and services please visit our website at http://www.clickthrough-marketing.com

ClickThrough Marketing can offer discounts on this book when ordered as a bulk purchase. For more information contact ClickThrough Marketing on 0800 088 7486 or email experts@clickthrough-marketing.com.

All images contained within this work are © iStockphoto.com.
Edited by John Newton.

Paid search is deceptively easy to start, but long-term success is challenging.

In our 101 Guide to pay per click marketing, you will find many practical tips, 101 in fact! So in the foreword I will highlight four of the most significant which, in my experience, are essential to successful pay per click marketing.

'Paid Search Requires Time And Dedication'

It's often said that in digital marketing, the 'devil is in the detail'. Nowhere is this more true than in paid search. A sound process is needed to manage potentially tens or even hundreds of thousands of keywords and to direct searchers to multiple landing pages on your site. Regular, in-depth, analysis and expertise in search and web analytics is essential to get the most from your campaign.

'Get Inside Your Customer's Mind'

We explain that understanding precisely what your customers are seeking, and which stage of the buying cycle they are in is essential to targeting searchers with relevant ads and effective landing pages. I always advise relative newcomers to paid search to look carefully at how searchers perceive your brand and isolate brand-terms when reporting account performance since these can skew analysis of campaign effectiveness.

'Long Tail Search Terms'

I agree with our comment that far too many companies focus on the most popular keywords and phrases and ignore specific targeting of the longer tail terms. Long tail terms are phrases which are four or more words long and lower volume, but potentially better quality traffic since the searcher is more advanced in selecting a product or service.

'The Importance Of Quality Score'

Many marketers who are new to paid search don't understand the importance of Quality Score in determining return on investment from paid search. Even if you're not managing paid search ads "hands-on", be sure to read our guidance on the importance of Quality Score and prompt the team managing paid search for you to report on how they are seeking to improve Quality Score.

So that's my take on four of the main factors needed to get value from your investment in paid search. I hope you find the many other pointers in our guide useful. All the best for refining your paid search!

Dr Dave Chaffey has been involved "hands-on" in SEM since 1998 when he built his first site. Since then he has consulted and trained many marketers to help improve their results from search engine marketing, including representatives from 3M, BP, HSBC Commercial, Mercedes-Benz, Smith and Nephew and Sony Professional.

Dave is also author of five best-selling business books including Internet Marketing: Strategy, Implementation and Practice; and eMarketing eXcellence (with PR Smith).

Phil Robinson is an online marketing consultant with over 16 years experience in marketing planning, internet strategy and online acquisition.

In 2004, Phil founded ClickThrough, an ethical search marketing agency specialising in pay per click, online PR, SEO, social media and conversion optimisation. He gives best practice training for businesses, runs seminars and writes eBooks on digital marketing strategy.

Lindsey Annison is ClickThrough's chief blogger. A practising internet marketing consultant since 1996, Lindsey helps companies improve their website marketing, online PR and information architecture. Lindsey is also a qualified adult education lecturer and author.

As co-founder of the Access to Broadband Campaign, she has been instrumental in the provision of high-speed internet access to rural areas in the UK. Lindsey is also a past winner of Silicon.com's "Outstanding Contribution to UK Technology"

ClickThrough
the search conversion experts

ClickThrough is an international search marketing and conversion optimisation consultancy. Since 2004 we have helped our clients in the UK, USA and Europe reach new customers in over 30 countries, using our proven, ethical search marketing know-how. We pride ourselves on giving honest, actionable advice without up-front commitments:

- ✓ No contract tie-ins for clients, giving you peace of mind.
- ✓ We link the remuneration of our people to client goals.
- ✓ Modular service offerings means we can be as flexible as you need.
- ✓ Proven track record from our work with clients including Peugeot, Vonage, Computeach, Norgren and DUO Boots.
- ✓ Our people all receive our industry-leading, Digital Academy training.
- ✓ Full account management team, with senior level contact for every client.
- ✓ Active members of the IAB, eConsultancy and SEMPO.
- ✓ Thought leaders, giving clients the inside track on what matters in search before it happens.

Whether you are thinking of changing your search or digital marketing agency, or just looking to improve your online conversion rate, our team of search conversion experts can help.

Find out what we can do to grow your business. Call us on **0800 088 7486** or visit **www.clickthrough-marketing.com**

What you will learn in this guide

ClickThrough
the search conversion experts

Introduction to PPC

#1 What Are SERPs?

SERPs (pronounced 'surps') are search engine results pages. When users type a search term into Google, a list of results show up for that term. The SERPs are made up of organic and paid results. Organic search results are the pages that the search engines feel are most relevant to your search request, based on hundreds of different factors.

A great website will list in the SERPs for hundreds, if not thousands, of different organic terms because of the high quality, keyword rich content they provide.

Quite often webmasters complain that they have lost their top SERPs ranking. Never focus on only one term or even just a handful of terms with your search engine marketing. Variety is the spice of search.

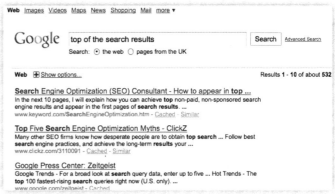

#2 Where Are The Paid Ads In SERPs?

The paid ads appear above the organic listings and on the right hand side too.
They are clearly identified as being different from the organic i.e. unpaid listings.

Each time a person views your advert, they generate an 'impression'. You do not pay for impressions (individual views of your advert) with PPC, but only when a user clicks the links within your ad.

#3 The Rise & Rise Of Google

In the early days of the web, no single search engine had a majority market share and many of the results returned were often irrelevant because of the simplicity of the search algorithms used. And then, in September 1998, Google Inc. was born.

Previously it had been very difficult to track down the information you were looking for.

Google made returning highly relevant results their first priority, which caught the attention of both web users and the media.

As more people began to use Google, the battle to be top of the SERPs became more competitive. 'Black hat' techniques were employed to con the search engines, who in turn developed more complex algorithms to establish 'relevance'. Pay per click advertising offered a fairer way to help companies appear at the top of search engine results, and provide much needed revenue for Google.

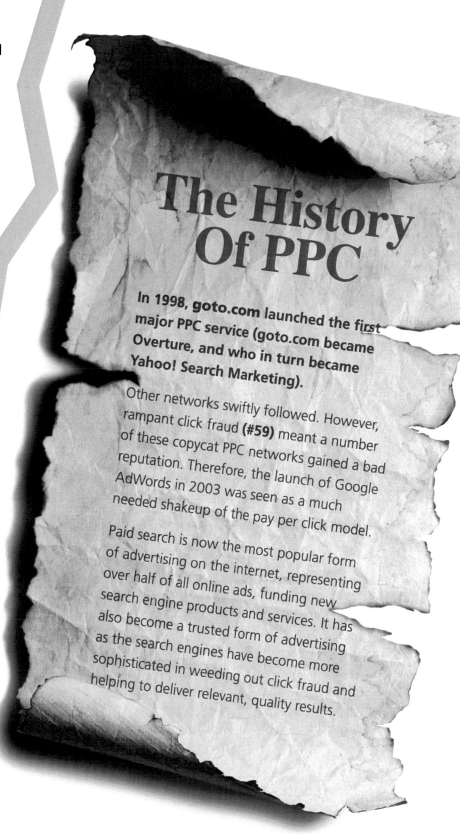

The History Of PPC

In 1998, goto.com launched the first major PPC service (goto.com became Overture, and who in turn became Yahoo! Search Marketing).

Other networks swiftly followed. However, rampant click fraud **(#59)** meant a number of these copycat PPC networks gained a bad reputation. Therefore, the launch of Google AdWords in 2003 was seen as a much needed shakeup of the pay per click model.

Paid search is now the most popular form of advertising on the internet, representing over half of all online ads, funding new search engine products and services. It has also become a trusted form of advertising as the search engines have become more sophisticated in weeding out click fraud and helping to deliver relevant, quality results.

#4 Key Pay Per Click Facts

AdWords is Google's version of Pay Per Click advertising. PPC allows you to bid (compete with other advertisers) on keywords and have your advert shown whenever a user submits a search query that includes one of your keywords. Your ad is then ranked according to a combination of elements, such as Quality Score, relevance and bid price.

- **Each advert consists of a mere 95 letters; 25 for the hyperlinked headline, 35 characters each for the two lines of the ad, plus 35 for the URL or link to your website.**

- **On Yahoo!, you are permitted 40 characters in the headline and 190 characters in the ad.**

- **On Bing, you are allowed the same as Google AdWords, with 1022 characters for the destination URL.**

Spending on PPC continues to rise, fuelled by the fact that, according to comScore, 2.9 million online searches are made every minute worldwide.

#5 Will Anyone Really Look At My Ad?

Despite claims that users ignore the paid listings in the SERPs, research shows that this is not true. This is supported by worldwide PPC spend, which was estimated at around £5bn in 2010.

Whilst a website visitor may screen out a banner advert, search engine listings will lead a buyer to the product or service they are seeking. This is particularly true later in the buying cycle, when your potential customer has acquired a clearer idea of precisely what they are seeking through their research.

However, even the smallest change to your ad can make a difference to whether it will be clicked on or not. Testing variants of adverts is vital to ensure that you maintain your Quality Score **(#66)** and get a return on investment from your PPC spend.

ClickThrough
the search conversion experts

Getting Started with PPC

Why Do You Want To Advertise?

It is important to establish what you are trying to achieve with your campaign before handing your credit card details to the search engines.

The results that you expect from such a campaign will define how you conduct it.

You may be looking to:

- **Test different search terms for optimisation purposes on your website.**
- **Offload spare stock quickly.**
- **Raise awareness of your brand in a competitive market place.**
- **Capture new sales or move into new markets.**

A scattergun approach will not work with PPC. Before planning a campaign, define your objectives rather than trying to be all things to all men.

#7 Key Steps Of PPC

To get started in PPC, there are a few important stages:

5 Adjust your bids, budget and adverts to improve results.

4 Monitor the search traffic and your rank.

3 Choose your keywords and write the text for your ads.

2 Await activation of your account.

1 Create an account and deposit funds (go to either **tinyurl.com/google-ppc-signup**, **tinyurl.com/yahoo-ppc-signup** or **tinyurl.com/microsoft-ppc-signup**).

We will explore many of these stages in detail, as you progress through this book.

the search conversion experts

#8 The Paid Search Model: Relevance, Bids and Customer Centricity

Paid search advertising has two main aims. The first is delivering relevant results for users. The second is to create value (revenue) for both the advertiser and the search engine. Both are important, and search engines will not compromise the appropriateness of their results just because an advertiser is prepared to pay more per click. Google's model of championing relevancy has become the industry standard and has now been adopted by Yahoo!, Microsoft and some second-tier (#87) networks.

It is always worth keeping the need for relevancy uppermost in your mind when writing ads. Choose the most relevant keywords for your copy and make sure you are bidding on keywords relevant to your products, services and landing pages.

Takeaways:
Pay per click rewards advertisers who focus on what the user requires, rather than just on hard *sell*. Keep your ads *customer-centric* and speak '*to them*', rather than '*about you*'.

#9 Paid Search Requires Time And Dedication

Most businesses today require their staff to multi-task, but some tasks can sometimes fall through the net. However, once started, a paid search campaign will run 24/7, spending your budget as it goes, regardless of its effectiveness - unless you take control. It is vital that you recognise the need to set aside time to monitor and manage your campaign from the outset, if you are to avoid unpleasant financial surprises at a later date.

Do not allow your campaign and bids to run out of hand, or you could lose money. Check your campaign each day during the first few months to make sure that you have not under or over-estimated the results you are able to achieve with your ads.

ClickThrough
the search conversion experts

#10 Don't Try To Trick The Search Engines

Google, Yahoo! and Microsoft have built their reputations and brands on quality and take a dim view of those who try to abuse their PPC products. Recently, Google removed 30,000 advertisers from AdWords for low quality ads. Whilst this could have a short-term effect on Google's revenue stream, it highlights how far the company will go to protect the user experience and thereby their reputation.

Get rich quick schemes are inevitably short-lived and trying to make a quick buck by finding ways around the stringent guidelines that the search engines set for their advertisers is likely to end in tears - yours.

#11 Organic & Paid Search: The Perfect Marriage

Obtaining prominent listings in both the PPC and organic results allows your site to be found on a multiplicity of search terms, and being seen in different places, sometimes twice on the same page, can create a big impact on your potential customers.

Some advertisers use the organic results to rank for key terms (reducing their PPC click costs on these major phrases), then add additional support by bidding on other terms using PPC. Other advertisers prefer to rank in both paid and organic results for their most important keywords, dominating the search results pages.

Takeaways:

For highly competitive terms, optimise pages within your site for SEO (search engine optimisation) in order to gain organic rankings where the PPC bid price may be uneconomical.

#12 Search And The Buying Cycle

Every purchase that you and your customers make is subject to a buying cycle; from initial need recognition, research, product selection and eventually purchase.

Some buying cycles can be very short e.g. a distress purchase buying flowers from a garage forecourt for a forgotten birthday. Other buying cycles can be much longer e.g. choosing the car that you drive to that same garage.

Understanding how your potential customers think during this cycle is vital.

It will mean the difference between maximising profits from marketing spend and losing money.

Create profiles of your customers at different stages of the buying process in order to find the different terms and keywords they use during each stage. You can then feed this right back into your campaign keywords and within your ads.

#13 The Self Selecting Potential Customer

Consumers have become more intelligent in the way they use search engines. Users are now more likely to use long-tail keywords (#21), using multi-word phrases to create product shortlists, to compare prices, and find discounts.

The hope of any online business is to survive this selection process and be visible as prospects' make their purchasing decisions. Consider different search terms to attract visitors in different stages of the buying cycle. For instance, a generic term such as "flat screen monitor" is an early interest search term. After some additional research, your potential customers' searches will become more defined. For instance, terms such as "widescreen", "plasma", brand names and model numbers will be used when a buyer is closer to making a purchase decision.

Takeaways: Focus on generic search terms to capture shoppers near the beginning of the buying cycle (the research phase). Use detailed search terms that describe your product to reach consumers who are closer to the end of the buying cycle.

the search conversion experts

#14 Get Inside Your Customer's Mind

Understanding precisely what your customers are seeking and which stage of the buying cycle they are in, will help you to create winning ads. Some customers may only care about price, others are looking for specific features, or will only buy from a company that they know and trust.

Map out the criteria that your customers may use when searching for, or researching, your products and services. Then, evaluate how you measure up against those criteria e.g. if you offer feature-rich products, make that a priority within your campaign. You can then identify all the terms that are associated with the criteria. Additionally, tools such as DoubleClick Ad Planner (owned by Google - **google.com/adplanner**) can help you understand the demographic makeup of the visitors to both your website and the sites belonging to your competitors. This in turn can be fed back into the planning stage of your campaign.

Preparing Your Campaign

#15 Keywords: Building Your Search Toolkit

Your keyword list will prove one of the most useful tools in your toolkit for both SEO and PPC.

Your keyword list should include hundreds, if not thousands, of terms. This should include long-tail terms: 4 or 5 word phrases which bring in smaller levels of traffic than the top keywords for your sector, business, products and services.

When creating your keyword list, think about all the terms a user may use when searching for your product. Brainstorm your keywords with colleagues, friends, customers, from your competitors' websites, with a thesaurus, and by searching online. Make sure to include new terms on both your site, as well in your ads, to increase your exposure in the rankings.

#16 Multiplying Your Keyword List

The search engines know that the larger your paid keyword list, the more you are likely to spend. To this end, they provide a number of tools to help expand your keyword list, exponentially.

The most popular of these tools is the Google Keyword Suggestion Tool (tinyurl.com/Google-Keyword-Suggestion-Tool), which can be used in plenty of ways to find new keywords:

- ☑ Enter the URL of a competitor's website to find the keywords suggested for their site, and add these to your keyword list.

- ☑ Start seeking 'broad match' terms and then narrow your focus to find more detailed terms.

- ☑ Use the keyword tool to group together related words within your campaign as suggested by Google at the top of the list.

- ☑ Spot seasonal trends by using the "Highest volume achieved in..." column.

For more suggestions, try the Wonder Wheel which can be found in the Options menu on a Google SERPs page. Microsoft offers their own suggestion tool at tinyurl.com/Microsoft-Keyword-Suggestion, as well as a well-supported, advanced tool that plugs into Microsoft Excel.

#17 Evolve Your Keyword List Over Time

There are multiple third-party keyword research tools, including wordtracker.com, seobook.com **and** keywordspy.com.

Use a variety of these tools to expand your campaign's keyword list. Keep all of your keywords in a spreadsheet. Your list will grow and evolve over time, as will hopefully your budget - add new keywords when you are comfortable that you can afford them.

ClickThrough
the search conversion experts

#18 Spy On Your Competitors' Campaigns

Legally

You should regularly review your competitors' campaigns, noting terms that you may have overlooked.

Tools such as ppcwebspy.com allow you to see what keywords your competitors are bidding on, and other tools like keywordspy.com can show the ad copy your rivals are using.

Use your keyword list to find your competitors' campaigns on the major search engines, and remember to look for foreign companies with an English language site. Your competition may no longer be on your doorstep now that you have entered the global marketplace.

#19 How To Find Keywords Others Have Missed

Misspellings and synonyms are the two most common forms of keywords that others may have ignored or forgotten.

Whilst Google corrects misspellings in the search box for the organic results, the inclusion of misspellings in your PPC campaign can provide low cost traffic with little competition.

Many website owners only focus on the top-performing keywords rather than digging deep to find the less frequently used phrases which will still bring in a steady stream of visitors over time.

#20 Choosing Keywords That Suit You

There is no point using keywords which attract high traffic numbers, if they do not describe your products and services.

Search engines will punish you for your lack of relevance, and you will waste both your prospects' time and your money.

For instance, if you sell accountancy services, you may want to bid on 'auditing services', 'chartered accountant', 'bookkeeping services', 'small business accounting', and 'tax planning' - but if you don't offer 'payroll services', don't add it to your keyword list.

Think particularly about the pain points that may have prompted a consumer's search in the first place. Remember that they may not be aware of the correct industry terminology, so use plain English as well as more technical terms.

#21 Long-Tail Search Terms

Far too many companies focus on the most popular keywords and phrases and ignore the longer tail terms.

These phrases are four or more words long and bring in constant, though lower volume, traffic over time. Including long-tail terms in your campaign can result in an improved conversion rate as you can use them to craft highly relevant landing pages that are much closer to the expectations of the searcher.

Prospects often use long-tail search terms when they are closer to the end of the buying cycle. For that reason, it is worthwhile adding them to your campaign. Finding long-tail terms can be as easy as running a search query report, to see the exact phrases that have triggered an ad view.

Long-tail terms can also be far cheaper as these niche terms often have very little competition. If you only focus on short, high-traffic terms you will find it hard to lower your own campaign cost per click.

#22 How To Put Keyword Budgets In Context

Without an idea of click costs, it can be difficult to put keywords into context. For this reason, Google introduced the Traffic Estimator tool (**tinyurl.com/google-trafficestimator**).

You can use this tool to understand likely positions (rankings) for different budgets, and also see the estimates for an unlimited budget by selecting "show total potential clicks".

It is important to use the estimator during the planning stages, particularly if you are on a low budget, in order to get maximum returns.

ClickThrough
the search conversion experts

#23 Setting Up Your AdWords Account

In order to start using AdWords you will first need a Google account. Users of Google Analytics will already have one in place, but setting up an account is easy; Google takes you through all of the steps required at tinyurl.com/New-AdWords-Account. The process is simple and should only take a few minutes.

Once you have an account, sign in to adwords.google.com to start your first campaign.

#24 Exploring The PPC Campaign Elements

There are various elements within a campaign. Here is what each one means:

Locations: choose which region or geographic territory you wish to target. It is best to start small e.g. target your home country first before attempting a global campaign.

Demographics: you can target specific age groups and gender. However, unless you are selling products which are only appropriate to a narrow range of people, it is better to reach the widest possible audience.

Networks and Devices: this advanced option allows you to target mobile devices, such as iPhones, as well as the content networks that Google owns or partners with.

Bidding and Budget options: you can choose between CPC (cost per click), CPA (cost per acquisition) and CPM (the cost of showing your ad to 1000 people).

Advanced Settings: these allow you to run a campaign for a specific time, as well as set caps on rotation **(#76)** and frequency (number of times someone sees your ad).

#25 PPC Ad Construction

A PPC ad has a number of different elements. Here is what to think about when creating your first ad:

Ad Creative Elements

Headline	**Only Three Lines Plus URL**
Lines of text aka "body text'	Easy to understand & clear benefits Tailored to customer buying cycle
Display URL	**http://put.keywords.in.copy.and.URL**
Destination URL	**http://goes.to.your.landing.page**

#26 Writing Your First Ad

Once you have opened your account you will be ready to set up your first campaign.

Your first ad will be the most daunting but remember the basic rules of customer centricity - the 4 Cs:

4 C's:

Catchy, competition-beating headline - look at your competitors for inspiration if needs be.

Compelling text - think as a customer.

Call to Action - phrases such as 'Book Now', 'Reserve', 'Sign up Today' and 'Order Now' get your prospect in a buying frame of mind.

Check the URL - the link should rarely, if ever, go to your home page. It must go to the page on your site that relates to the product or service you are advertising.

#27 Standing Out From The Crowd

Your USPs (Unique Selling Points) should help you stand out from the crowd. For instance, type any competitive term into a search engine and look at the results.

How do you, as a potential customer, decide which of the listings is for you? Ads at the top are receiving higher clickthroughs. What benefits are they offering to the consumer?

Your USP is something you, and only you, can offer. Subjective rather than objective statements e.g. "the best" will require independent verification on your landing page (your destination URL), so be careful.

USPs should be customer, rather than seller, focussed. For instance, free delivery can be a big selling point if your competitors charge for shipping.

#28 Adopt Your Customer's Tone

By profiling your audience you can better understand their needs and concerns. What makes YOU tick or click? What ads draw your attention? Analyse why they work for you. It is far easier to write an advert that you believe in.

So, for instance, if your products are for the younger demographic, you need to use language which will resonate with that audience. If you are dealing with business buyers, you should give details which will help them to make a purchasing decision - price, specifications and so on. Always bear in mind however that you may not be a typical customer so ask others what makes them click too.

Once written, test your ads by targeting at specific demographics using the advanced features of the AdWords campaign manager.

ClickThrough
the search conversion experts

#29 Create Powerful, Keyword Rich Headlines

Headlines are the most important part of any PPC ad.

A good headline will intrigue a customer enough so that they read the rest of your ad, and clickthrough to your site.

Here are some tactics to consider when crafting a PPC headline:

- Ensure that your keywords are in your headline. Google will bold them, which will draw the eye, and improve your Quality Score.

- Want to know how to make a great headline? Then ask a question. Questions challenge the consumer, especially if they reflect the pain point **(#20)** that prompted their search.

- Capitalise Every Word To Stand Out.

- You can use your headline to pre-qualify your visitors. If you offer a high quality business card printing service, the headline "Premium Business Cards" will pull in a less price-conscious audience than "Cheap Business Cards".

Takeaways:

An ad with a great headline but poor body copy will almost always perform better than an ad with strong body copy but a lacklustre headline.

#30 Using Action Words

In Your Body Text

Your body text needs to follow on from the headline and persuade your reader to click on your link.

Action words are the key here, such as 'Discover', 'Find', 'Send', 'Get' and 'Download'.

It is usually better to break your body text into smaller sentences. Rather than write "If you order your photos today you get up to 50% off & free delivery" try "Up to 50% off all Photo Processing. Free Delivery. Order today!"

#31 Your Display URL: The Gift Of An Extra Line For Copy

Your display URL is often the last thing a prospect sees before they decide whether to click on your ad.

After spending time crafting a concise, attractive ad the temptation is to use your root domain e.g. 'your-companys-site.com' as the display URL. Doing so would throw away the gift of an 'extra line' of text to get your message across.

Careful use of keywords within your display URL can reiterate your message e.g. 'your-companys-site.com/free-expert-advice' and prompt clickthrough.

However, you need to employ URL redirection so that if anyone types this URL into the address bar it will still take them through to the correct landing page. You must also ensure that the domain in your display URL matches that used in your destination URL.

#32 Trimming Down Your Ads

At first, you may find fitting your message into 95 characters a challenge. However, with practice you can learn how to use the minimum amount of space whilst standing out from the crowd. Here are some pointers:

• Remove all unnecessary words e.g. 'we', 'in', 'on', 'it', 'of' and 'the'.

• Use the thesaurus to find shorter alternatives of words e.g. 'extensive' becomes 'huge' and 'request' becomes 'get'.

• Where allowed, use abbreviations or truncations when possible e.g. 'hours' becomes 'hrs' and 'pictures' becomes 'pics'.

• Use numbers instead of words. e.g. '£50' instead of 'fifty pounds'.

• Focus on the benefits of your product or service, avoiding hyperbole.

• Use the ampersand (&) instead of 'and' to save precious space.

Takeaways:

Creating short, powerful ads is an art form. For this reason, many clients' let their agencies write their ads for them.

#33 Using Incentives As Bait

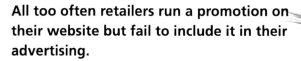

All too often retailers run a promotion on their website but fail to include it in their advertising.

To increase traffic, remember to include your on-site offers in your ads. You should also keep an eye on promotions that your competitors are running - where it makes commercial sense, aim to beat their best deal too.

There are regulatory and legal obligations to observe when employing incentives in advertising. Avoid incentives that you are unable to deliver on, or which are stretching the reality of the offer e.g. 'free' offers that require additional purchases.

#34 Why Punctuation Matters

An effective ad is all about appearance; and imaginative use of punctuation can help your ad stand out:

• An exclamation mark can emphasise the importance of a particular offer e.g. 'Fast free shipping!'

• The use of the 'pipe' (|) character can force the user to pause while reading your ad e.g. 'Genuine Printer Inks | Next Day Delivery'.

• For a really striking effect, use full stops creatively e.g. "Fastest. Worldwide. Delivery. Guaranteed.".

• Whilst Many People Dislike The Capitalisation Of Every Word In A Sentence, It Has Been Proven To Be Effective In Many Tests.

• You can also use TM, © and ® characters to show that your site is the official website for your brand.

#35 Dynamic Keyword Insertion

This powerful feature can alter your ad to reflect the user's search term.

So, for instance, if your ad group is for Motorbikes, the keyword insertion tag can insert Honda, Kawasaki, Ducati, Yamaha, Suzuki into either the headline, the copy or the URL. All you need do is to indicate where you want the appropriate term placed.

For example, if your ad title is:
Buy {keyword:motorbikes} bikes online

Keyword:	Ad Title shown as:
Yamaha	Buy Yamaha bikes online
Suzuki	Buy Suzuki bikes online
Ducati	Buy Ducati bikes online

What if you want to capitalise the First Letter Of Every Word? You can do this automatically too.

{keyword:xyz} will show your keyword(s) in lower case

{KeyWord:xyz} will capitalize the first letter of each word

the search conversion experts

#36 Stay Within The Rules

The major search engines are very good at providing full and complete guidelines and rules.

Whilst these may be complex, understanding them will help to ensure that you do not inadvertently break a rule, the penalty for which can be ad rejection.

Whilst it may seem difficult to keep up with all the changes affecting PPC advertisers, we strongly recommend that you read the T&Cs thoroughly, work with your agency or PPC manager to ensure you are within the guidelines, and you can also keep up to date by subscribing to the various blogs and Twitter feeds that the main PPC engines maintain.

#37 Dealing With Ad Rejection

Google may reject an ad for display if their guidelines have not been adhered to.

There are several reasons for disapproved ads, and it is usually a simple matter to change the offending item and resubmit.

For instance, make sure you are only using a single URL within an ad group. Unsuitable or inappropriate content is another reason. Check which of the Google Terms and Conditions your content breaches, and change your campaign to comply with their guidelines.

Google has a long list of prohibited goods and services for which AdWords is off-limits.

These can be found at **tinyurl.com/Google-Advertising-Policies** and include gambling, alcohol, pharmaceuticals, tobacco and other sensitive issues. Microsoft offer a tool that can detect whether a page is likely to be seen as 'sensitive' by search engines (**tinyurl.com/Microsoft-Sensitive-Site-Tool**).

Advanced Keyword Usage

ClickThrough
the search conversion experts

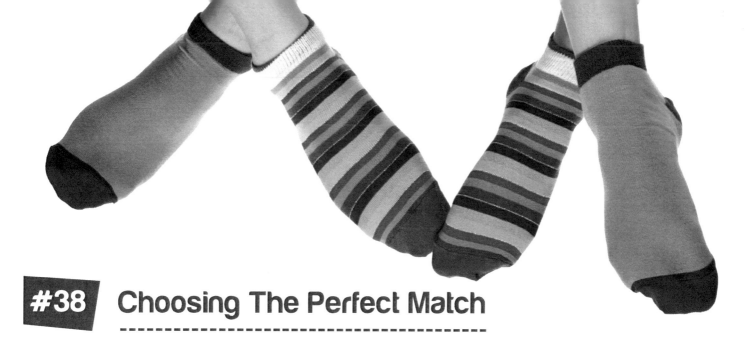

#38 | Choosing The Perfect Match

All three major search engines use matching technologies to pair your ad with user searches.
Understanding how keyword matching works is important to achieve the right blend between traffic volume and relevancy.

- **Exact match** will show your ad when the search query matches your search phrase or term exactly.

- **Broad match** allows your ad to be triggered by other relevant phrases as well as your own keyword choices; this is the default setting for AdWords.

- **Phrase match** will show your ad when one of your keywords appears somewhere within the search term entered.

- **Negative match** will ensure that your ad is not shown for any search that includes that keyword.

Whilst you may receive fewer clickthroughs with exact match, the traffic is more likely to be highly targeted than with broad match.

#39 Broad Match - Friend Or Foe?

Around 25% of the searches made by users worldwide each month have never been made by anyone before.

Broad match (also known as 'Advanced Match') uses computing power to serve ads that are relevant to these brand new search queries. However, there are often occasions when broad match will show your ad in unrelated searches. If this results in a reduced clickthrough rate, this will impact on your Quality Score.

You can reduce the likelihood of your ad showing for irrelevant searches by:

a) Only using broad match on longer tail **(#21)** search terms.

b) Identifying non-relevant terms and adding these to your negative keyword list **(#40)**.

Remember that increasing impressions - e.g. using broad match - may look good in your stats, but using longer tail terms or exact match will look good on your bottom line and hence increase profits.

Employing Negative Keywords

Keyword negatives give you another way of controlling the type of traffic that your PPC campaign delivers by filtering out irrelevant search terms.

If you look through your Analytics account you may be surprised at some of the unusual search queries that have resulted in a visit to your site. By building up a robust negative keyword list, you can reduce your overall spend by 10-20% whilst maintaining your number of conversions by weeding out irrelevant traffic. For example:

- If you offer a premium product, look to add discount-related keywords to your negative list e.g. 'free', 'cheap', 'bargain', 'samples', 'voucher' and 'surplus'. Software providers may also consider the term 'open source' and music retailers the word 'lyrics'.

- A lot of searches also include the name of major websites. Unless your product is directly related to these companies, filter out these names through your negatives list e.g. facebook, ebay, craigslist and amazon.

- Add careers-related negatives to your list to minimise visits from job seekers e.g. 'opportunities', 'recruitment', 'jobs' and 'vacancies'.

- Unless data is your business, consider adding research-related keywords to your negatives list e.g. 'statistics', 'case studies', 'data', 'guides' and 'reviews'.

- If you offer a fully-finished product, filter out those who are looking to do it for themselves e.g. 'recipes', 'patterns', 'tutorial', 'crafts' and 'homemade'.

- Some users are looking to learn about your market rather than buy. Unless you run courses, filter out the following keywords; 'classes', 'course', 'training' and 'college'.

Takeaways:

By using negative keywords in your campaign, you can target your spend at people in the market to buy, and get more accurate statistics about conversions, bounce rates (the number of people leaving your site after viewing only one page), and the effectiveness of your ads.

the search conversion experts

Group Similar Keywords Together To Test Performance

When creating ad groups, it is a good idea to keep related terms together.

#41

This allows you to isolate the combined performance of similar keywords and pause seasonal ad groups when events are over e.g. Easter, Valentines.

Remember, your Quality Score will be affected by the different terms within each ad group so by grouping keywords together in this way you will also keep your Quality Score high, and bid costs low.

#42 Seeking Out Extra Variants Of Your Keywords

Google will offer different results for singular and plural keywords, so bid on both terms and put them on your website.

You should also practice stemming - looking for all variants of a word. This can include verbs, participles, adverbs, and so on.

For instance, you may offer a book publishing service. In which case, you need to consider bidding on the words 'publisher', 'publishers', 'publication', 'publish', 'published' and 'publications' as well as your major keyphrase 'publishing service'. Think and optimise beyond the 'top' keyword. Invariably your customers will too.

#43 Dealing With Underachieving Keywords

The best thing to do when a keyword or phrase is under-achieving is to either remove it from the campaign, or try to rewrite the ad.

You may also find that it is not your ad which is under-performing, but your website and in particular, landing pages. Take another look at your site structure, copy and landing pages to ensure that these are as effective as they should be.

Remember that low performing keywords can affect your overall Quality Score for your account.

ClickThrough
the search conversion experts

#44

Expanding Your Keyword List

You should constantly be adding to your keyword list, and creating corresponding ads and ad groups, to stay ahead of the pack.

- Write down your keywords each time you think of a new one - keep a pen and paper by your bed!

- Use Google Insights (google.com/insights/search/) to get real data about search trends.

- Expand your list with Microsoft's Advertising Intelligence Tool (tinyurl.com/ microsoft-intelligence-tool) which plugs in to Excel 2007 and is specifically designed to help with keyword expansion and selection.

As well as the search engines use third-party tools such as adgooroo.com, speedppc.com, joojab.com and wordstream.com to find related additional long-tail keywords you may have overlooked. Another useful tool is seodigger.com which will show high-performing organic keywords for your site, which can then be fed into your PPC campaign.

Running Your Campaign

#45 Fine Tuning Your Campaign

With regular monitoring of your campaign you will be able to spot under-performing keywords, reduce bids, and get a better return on investment.

The Search Query Report will enable you to discover all the terms that have been searched upon and you should run a report at least once a week, or ask your agency to do so. These can then be fed back into your campaign and new ads created.

By finding new, relevant keywords for your campaign you can boost your Quality Score and ensure you are paying the minimum bid for position.

ClickThrough
the search conversion experts

#46 Choosing The Right Time Of Day To Reach Your Audience

"Day parting" is a technique with origins in broadcast media, where advertisers will specify the time of day when their ads should appear e.g. targeting housewives during the daytime, or kids in weekend morning childrens' programming.

This same technique can be applied to your PPC campaign. For example, your audience may be more likely to buy during natural breaks in their day e.g. lunchtime, rather than in a five minute mid-morning break.

Save money by reducing bids during quiet periods, and boosting them when your prospects are most active. For example, Yahoo! offers a 'daily planner' visualisation where you can easily highlight blocks of time and then adjust bids across the campaign.

#47 Browse On Sunday, Buy On Monday

In many sectors, especially B2B markets, prospects lose the buying mindset at the weekend. Searches decrease, and conversion rates drop. You can save funds by reducing or pausing your ads on these days.

Conversely, many people use weekends and evenings to shop for items that they do not have time to consider on weekdays such as hobby related purchases. Some prospects research purchases on Sunday to buy as a Monday lunchtime pick-me-up.

By being active at the same time as your customers you can put your budget to best use.

#48 Controlling Expectations: Tying Your Stock Levels To Your AdWords Account

How many times have you clicked on an ad for a specific item only to find it is out of stock? Out of stock items result in wasted consumer time, and unnecessary PPC spend. Don't fall into this trap.

Remove any out of stock products from your PPC campaign by pausing the relevant ads until you have restocked. Some e-commerce and bidding systems can automate this process. This will save your money, and prevent potential customer disappointment.

ClickThrough
the search conversion experts

29

#49 Learning How To Manage Your Budget

Setting your PPC budget can be difficult. Although you will want to avoid wasted money, you also need a steady stream of clicks through to your site to understand what works. Choose a figure that you can live with, given the likely level of clicks it will generate.

When starting out, you may be inclined to divide your budget up equally across each ad group. However, it's better to divide your budget using the estimated data you have collected on likely search volumes and bid costs for the keywords within each ad group. This can stop some ad groups being starved of budgets while other groups fail to spend even a fraction of their own. Once you have actual campaign data, redistribute your spend to the areas that have performed the best.

Takeaways:

Careful evaluation of each ad group, both initially and on an ongoing basis, will help you determine how to best apportion your ad budget.

#50 Why Being Top Isn't Always The Name Of The Game

Recent tests show that the clickthrough rate (CTR) by position in the search rankings varies widely.

For instance, ads in Position 1 may achieve a CTR of 3%, whereas those in Position 2 could receive half that number. However, although ads lower down the page usually achieve a lower CTR, they can often have a higher conversion rate, as they are more likely to be clicked on by serious prospects who have taken time to read each ad. It is worthwhile to test how your ad converts at different positions by using position preferencing **(#77)**.

Some search engines will allow a different number of ads per page (for example, Yahoo! will often show twelve ad results per page) so you will need to adjust your bids accordingly.

ClickThrough
the search conversion experts

Hold The Front Page: First Page Bids

Google gives advertisers a minimum bid price for any keyword they wish to bid on. However, this doesn't give any indication of position within the search results for that term.

Given that the first page of results receives 90% of clicks, this is a serious omission, and one that Google has now rectified. Google now gives a first page bid estimate - the price that you will need to pay to have a strong chance of appearing on page 1 for a search term.

It's worth increasing the suggested first page bid estimate by 15% in order to rank higher than just the tenth position. Additionally, aim to secure a high-ranking first page spot for long-tail terms - it is these searchers who are already part way down the buying funnel.

#52 Putting A Price On Your Customer Relationships

Your maximum CPCs should be based on fact, not gut-feel. By understanding your average basket size, conversion rate and profit margins you can estimate the likely return from a visit to your site, and hence the maximum price you could pay per click.

Some businesses operate a 'lifetime customer value' model, which estimates the total amount of revenue that a customer will bring in during their relationship with a website.

These predicted numbers can help you appreciate the long term value that a PPC click can deliver. An ad click that is unprofitable when viewed in the context of the initial visit, may become vastly profitable when additional sales are taken into account. Remember, once a visitor gives you their email address they can be marketed to very inexpensively.

Here is an example:

You sell a product with a £10 profit margin. Your conversion rate is 2% i.e. for every 100 visitors, 2 of them buy your product. Therefore, for 100 visitors you make £20. This means you can afford to spend up to 20p per click to attract visitors and still break even. If you decide to bid more than 20p for that keyword you will have to either increase your conversion rate or increase the price of your products.

#53 Let Google Do Your Bidding

If you are just starting out, or are unsure of the right bidding strategy, you can allow Google to bid automatically for you. Simply set a daily budget and Google will seek out the maximum number of clicks for you using their Budget Optimizer. However, whilst this may save time initially, Google will not necessarily know which of your products are generating the most profit per click. For that reason it is best to employ automatic bidding only when you are seeking a simple response from visitors to your site e.g. a form fill landing page, and then incorporate any findings back into your campaign.

#54 Don't Let Your Competitors Drag You Down With Them

Just because one of your competitors has decided to bid over the odds for a keyword doesn't mean that you need to follow. Bid according to the results you receive, rather than aiming to beat your competitors, who could be overbidding.

Tools such as keywordspy.com will give you in-depth information on your competitors' PPC campaigns, including their overall click costs. Could you make a profit at the price they are paying? Then, turn your attention to your own campaign. Are there any unprofitable keywords that you could cull? It is perfectly feasible that your competitors are overbidding to try to beat YOU on unprofitable terms, pushing up prices further.

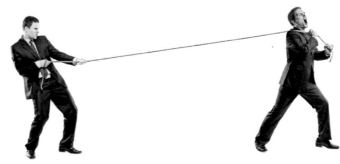

#55 Every Keyword Should Stand On Its Own Two Feet

Each keyword that you bid on needs to be profitable in its own right. Rather than setting bids on a group or campaign level, make bid changes at the keyword level. Every keyword is subject to differing levels of competition and traffic volumes, and needs to be viewed in isolation.

Once again, it is important to run reports so that you are aware of how each of your top keywords are performing in order to tweak your bids to reflect performance and payback.

ClickThrough
the search conversion experts

#56 Using Bid Management Tools

If you are finding day-to-day management a struggle, you may want to start using a bid management tool. These provide a single point of access to all your campaigns across multiple search engines, and contain complex automated bidding technology which can save you both time and money.

Each tool has different benefits. If you are only using Google for your PPC, then you could consider Google's Conversion Optimizer but you will need to have had at least 15 conversions in the last 30 days.

However, if you are working across multiple networks then other tools can help. Correct setup is vital, which is why many advertisers work with agencies to run their bid management for them. Where possible, seek advice from others but be prepared for many different answers - this a growing market and new tools appear daily.

#57 Winning The Impression Share Battle

If your ads are not appearing when you expect them to, it is likely that you have lost impression share.

To find out what impression share you are receiving, run a Campaign Performance report within your AdWords account. Make sure that 'Impression Share', 'Lost IS (Rank)', 'Lost IS (Budget)' and 'Exact Match IS' options are checked.

Where you have lost share, the reason will be given in the next two columns. This will be down to insufficient budget, or because your low ranking meant that your competitors pushed you off the page.

'Exact Match IS' means the percentage of times your ad was shown as a result of someone typing in the exact keywords you are bidding on. If Google is not convinced that your ads are relevant even for an exact match, you should be concerned. If your 'Exact Match IS' is low (e.g. under 75%) then you need to review every aspect of your campaign (ads, landing page, load time, bids etc) in turn.

#58 Managing Your Account Offline

Most PPC advertisers begin by operating their accounts through the online interface provided by the search engines. However, as accounts grow they can become unwieldy. For this reason, the search engines now offer desktop applications that give more advanced users the opportunity to reduce the time needed to make campaign wide changes.

Google offers the AdWords Editor (tinyurl.com/Google-Desktop-Editor), Yahoo! have their Search Marketing Desktop (tinyurl.com/Yahoo-Desktop-Editor) and Microsoft provides advertisers with their adCenter Desktop (tinyurl.com/Microsoft-Desktop-Editor).

One major benefit of these tools is the ability to download campaigns to Excel. Changes can then be made en masse (e.g. increasing bids, replacing certain phrases etc) and then uploaded to the search engine in one go. Experienced users will often build an entire campaign in Excel, only uploading to the search engine when they are ready to submit it for approval. For those working within a group, entire accounts can be downloaded to one file that can then be shared with, and reviewed by, other group members.

Takeaways:

As with any advanced software tools, they need to be used with care. However, in the hands of professionals these desktop editors can free up time for creativity and innovation.

#59 What Is Click Fraud?

Click fraud occurs when someone clicks on your ad maliciously (to spend your budget) without any intention of buying your product.

All the search engines are fully aware of this practice and do their best to stamp it out. Most click fraud is malicious in intent - attempting to frame a competitor or owner of a website hosting the ads. Some click fraud can be well meaning, but misguided e.g. your staff thinking that clicking on your ads will help increase CTR and hence your rankings.

- **Click fraud is big business, with a number of 'click farms' (groups of people paid to click on ads) already established in developing countries.**

- **Webmasters may be tempted to click on the PPC ads on their site to boost their revenue.**

- **There are also a number of computer scripts aka 'bots' that emulate real users, clicking on ads.**

According to the global Click Fraud Index, 15.3% of all clicks in Q4 2009 were click fraud attempts, so you should monitor your campaign carefully and report any suspicious instances of multiple clicks from the same IP address.

the search conversion experts

#60 How To Make Your Campaign Pay For Itself

Each campaign you run can be fine-tuned to ensure that it pays for itself:

- **Ads** - Write new ads based on your findings. Then, once they have established themselves, delete your old ads. Following the process in this order helps protect your Quality Score.

- **Landing Pages** - Aim for a clear call to action, fast load times, precise text and lack of clutter.

- **Your Website** - Make sure your e-commerce engine and shopping basket are fast and efficient; that you have reliable hosting; and great on-site content.

- **Back Office** - Ensure that your customer service, order processing, shipping, and complaints procedure is first class. This will help reduce credit card chargebacks and encourage repeat custom.

Landing pages should help prospects find the answers they are seeking as quickly as possible. Landing Page Quality (LPQ) will also determine your position in the rankings. The main criteria are:

- **Relevancy - pertinent, original content.**
- **Openness - providing contact details for your business.**
- **Respect - for your visitors' details, computers and privacy.**
- **Navigability - make your site and landing pages easy to use.**

Learn about which landing pages are more effective by testing them using Google's Website Optimizer (google.com/websiteoptimizer) and by learning from the experiences of other webmasters e.g. whichtestwon.com. You can also test the load time of your landing page using tools such as fiddler2.com or tinyurl.com/yahooslow

#62 Filtering Out Visitors Who Refuse To Convert

The majority of people who click on your ads will fail to convert. Analytics programs will track a visitor from the point of entry through to goal completion, and you can use this information to understand which keywords are bringing in more sales.

Work out which keywords bring 'spectators' to your site rather than customers. Tailor your ads and keywords to target genuine potential customers, rather than lurkers.

Takeaways:

Once you understand who is visiting and buying from your site, you can change the language or offers used in your ad to weed out those who don't.

ClickThrough
the search conversion experts

#63 Following Up With Your Prospects

Whilst not all visitors to your site will give their contact details, you should follow up on all those prospects that have. Once a visitor has made a conscious decision to investigate your site, you are part way to conversion.

Email and phone enquiries should be dealt with promptly. Ask your prospects how they would prefer to be contacted. Some may prefer to correspond via Twitter, or be part of a forum or social network. Use surveys and feedback forms to gather this information and record it as their preference in your CRM database.

#64 How Business And Consumer Search Differs

Business searchers (B2B) will frequently use industry-specific terminology, have a much longer buying cycle, and are likely to shop around - their job depends on it. A successful visit to a B2B website could result in a form fill, phone call, webinar registration or face-to-face meeting. In contrast, consumer searches (B2C) are more likely to end in an immediate online purchase.

Although B2C brands frequently talk about establishing a relationship with consumers, this is usually a goal of the supplier, rather than the customer. B2B customers are far more likely to want to establish a long-term relationship with a supplier, rather than a one off deal. The triggers for B2B customers are therefore different to those for B2C and your ads need to be worded accordingly.

B2B landing pages should be designed to get that relationship off on the right foot, and whilst these pages may include your sales pitch, your contact details need to be equally prominent.

#65 Pay For Performance

By understanding the acceptable CPA (cost per acquisition) for each sale, you will be able to adjust your PPC bids with more confidence. This will also stop you over-bidding on terms which, although attractive, fail to convert. Use Google's Bid Simulator to calculate the profit you can expect to make from different CPA bids. You may find that you can decrease your bid, and increase your profitability.

Google recognises that many advertiser's would prefer to pay a set fee for each conversion, rather than pay per click. A number of their latest products e.g. Product Ads (which draws upon Google Base product feeds) now offer a cost-per-acquisition model. However, Google still takes into account the Quality Score of the advertiser's website when deciding which ads to show. Google also runs an Affiliate Network (**google.com/ads/affiliatenetwork**), which works on a CPA basis.

ClickThrough
the search conversion experts

The Importance of Quality Score

#66 Quality Score: Google's Long Term Memory

Quality Score is a key factor in determining your position in the results, and also in helping you to achieve a lower bid price for a higher listing. Your historical performance is considered by Google in determining your Quality Score, so you should endeavour to maintain a high CTR (clickthrough rate) across all of your keywords.

High volume keywords such as brand names will help increase your CTR and therefore bidding on your own brand should be a permanent part of your PPC strategy.

#67 Quality Score Factors

Almost every aspect of your AdWords account has a Quality Score (QS). This includes:

- **Keyword Quality Score** - your keyword Quality Score is combined with your maximum bid to determine the position of your ads for specific keywords.

- **Ad Group Quality Score** - the Quality Score of each ad group depends on the historical performance of the keywords it contains and the landing page quality.

- **Account Quality Score** - your account Quality Score is the sum of the historical performance of all your keyword Quality Scores.

Your keyword QS is made up of different elements. For instance, the relevance of your ad to your keywords; the clickthrough rate (recent CTR is prioritised, although lifetime clickthrough also carries certain weight); the account QS; and some geotargeting (location) and other relevancy factors.

Maintaining your Quality Score should be a key performance factor in your PPC campaign, and will be a focus for any agency that you work with.

ClickThrough
the search conversion experts

#68 The Quality Score Magic Formula

The Quality Score for your site is calculated from the relevance of the search to your ad, the historic clickthrough rate and landing page factors - how fast the page loads and the value of its content. This is just a part of the algorithm used to decide which ads show for a specific search. That keyword QS algorithm can be described as:

The price of your bid = (the next highest bid below you X the Quality Score of that ad) ÷ your Quality Score.

The higher you can maintain your Quality Score, the lower your bid will be. Both Yahoo! and Microsoft have their own version of Quality Score, with Microsoft also rewarding ads for their 'uniqueness' versus their competitors' ads.

Takeaways:

You cannot control the advert of the next bidder but by understanding this formula you can profit from their low Quality Scores.

#69 The Virtuous Circle Of Putting Searchers First

Search engines believe that if they put consumers first, the benefit to advertisers will follow. Getting consumers through to advertisers' websites as quickly as possible is part of that process; it benefits the consumer, the search engine (who are seen as delivering fast, effective search results) and the advertiser (who will reduce the likelihood of the visitor leaving their site before it has time to load).

Poor quality landing pages, irrelevant copy, or being sent to the home page instead of directly to the product page will also negatively affect your PPC campaign. PPC is not just about writing a 95 character ad. It is a complex combination of factors which will see you succeed or fail. This is where a good agency can often make all the difference.

#70 Using Keywords Throughout The User Journey

When a prospect clicks on your ad, they expect to find more about the product or service you have been advertising. You need to ensure that the keywords you use are hitting the right buttons for your visitor. Your first opportunity to attract their attention is the headline of your ad. This is followed by the body text, then the URL and then the landing page. At each point during this journey, you need to ensure that the keywords used clearly signpost that they are following the right route towards their goal.

Takeaways:

By repeating the keywords that triggered the ad in both your landing page, and the ad itself, you give the consumer confidence that your site will answer their needs.

Brands and Search

In addition to driving traffic to your site, pay per click can also increase brand awareness. From ensuring that your ads appear for searches on your own name, to 'owning' certain key phrases by always appearing in their top position, paid search can be a powerful branding tool.

#71

How PPC Can Help To Make Your Brand Famous

- Appearing in both organic and paid results has a bigger impact on prospects, which reflects well on your brand.

- Even if prospects don't click on your ads this time, they may remember your name and search on your brand name next time.

- Contextual advertising programs, such as AdSense, can put your PPC text ads in front of people as they spend time reading content online. Remember, the aim is to spend as little time as possible on a search results page, whereas the opposite is often true on other sites.

ClickThrough
the search conversion experts

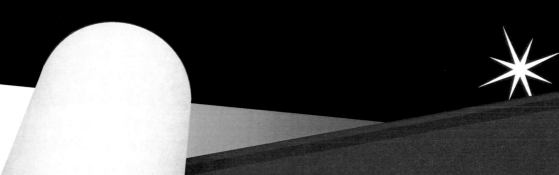

It is difficult to measure the value of raising brand awareness because it is a lifetime value rather than a quick win. Nevertheless, you should ensure that your key messages are consistent and that they reinforce your brand image at every opportunity.

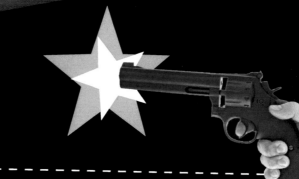

#72 Brand Bidding And Hijacking

The usage of brands within PPC took a new turn in May 2008 when Google announced that it would permit bidding on brand name keywords within the UK, although the use of trademark terms would remain prohibited. This meant that companies could potentially hijack traffic from searches on their competitors' brand names. Within two months Hitwise reported a 22% increase in paid search activity by the UK's top 100 brands.

There are potential legal problems if you bid on brands which are not your own. However, brand bidding can result in higher volumes of traffic and if you have relevant landing pages (because you sell, even if you don't own, the brand being bid on) it can even improve your Quality Score.

TESTING YOUR
W A Y   T O
S U C C E S S

A   J   K   D   J   H   Z

M   O   E   N   T   W   V

J   S   F   O   R   I   P   A

#73 | ## Turbo-Boost Results By Testing Your Ad Creative

You should never put up an ad and then sit back on your laurels. Testing, testing and more testing is the recipe for success. Without testing you will never know if your campaign is at its optimum.

Quite often, even a simple change to your ad creative can bring noticeable results. You can run tests from within AdWords, in Yahoo! Search Marketing and Microsoft adCenter, and then monitor the results of making those changes.

There are two main types of testing - A/B split testing and multivariate testing.

#74 A/B Split Testing

A/B testing involves testing one ad creative (labelled 'A') directly against another ('B'), one of which will act as a 'control'.

One risk with A/B testing is that your unproven test ad will take half of all available ad views, opportunities which may have been better utilised by your proven control creative. To minimise risk, create multiple copies of your control ad. Rather than being in a 50/50 rotation, your test would now be in a 20/20/20/20/20 rotation, assuming you create 3 copies of your control (i.e. the new ad, the original itself and its three copies).

If your test ad shows early promise, ramp up the pressure by deleting one of the copies of your control so that your test ad is then shown 25% of the time. If it is still performing, then delete another copy of the control, and so on. Conversely, if your test fails to perform you can delete both the new test ad and all copies of the control, except the original.

This modified version of traditional A/B testing ensures that your tests are well managed, without risking the traffic that your existing ads already bring in.

#75 Testing More Than One Thing At Once

Results from A/B tests can be gathered quickly. However, you may want to test more than one change at the same time. This technique is called 'multivariate' testing, and it can take some time to gather statistically relevant results. For example, you may wish to test how different body copy works with multiple headlines, or a range of display URLs. Firstly, aim to...

KISS - Keep It Simple, Stupid.

The number of different combinations with even a simple three line ad increases exponentially the more you wish to test. For instance, two versions of each of the three lines will give you 8 adverts to test, three versions of each line will give you 27 ads to test, and so on.

Secondly, think about how the two lines of text complement both each other and the headline. Make sure that the calls to action within your test headlines do not conflict with or duplicate word-for-word those in the body text.

It is possible to group together results from multivariate tests, for example to identify and aggregate instances where the same headline and body text was used, but where the display URL was different. Adding tests together in various patterns like this can help identify when two elements work together well, and by combining these results, help you to arrive at a 'champion' ad that much quicker.

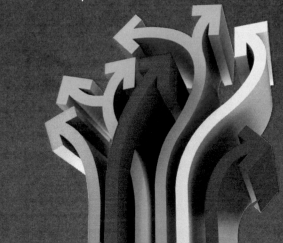

Rotating Your Ads

The default setting for ad rotation within AdWords is to show the highest performing ad in each group in preference to other ads in the group. Yahoo! also offers the same feature and you can set Ad Optimization as either 'on' or 'off'. Whilst this may seem to be a good thing, it doesn't give less frequently shown ads the opportunity they need to prove themselves over time.

You can switch off ad rotation so that all ads in a group are shown a similar number of times. This will help you to judge for yourself which ad creative is performing the best. Once each ad has been shown a statistically significant number of times you will be able to choose which ads should be flagged for deletion at a later date. You can then let Google make the decisions again, until you next have time to run an ad creative test.

#77 Choosing The Right Position For Your Ads

Often the optimal mix of clickthroughs and conversions will occur when your ads appear lower down the page (e.g. 3-6). However, you may find that in order to ensure your ads appear as often as possible you have to set a high maximum CPC (cost per click), which results in your ads appearing at the top of the page.

To help advertisers achieve this balancing act more easily, Google introduced Position Preferencing. This allows advertisers to set a range of positions in which they would be happy for their ads to appear. As long as your bid is high enough to allow you to appear within this range, your ad will appear.

For example, you may set a range of 3-8. Should your maximum bid be high enough to allow you to appear in the top positions e.g. 1-2, Google will reduce your bid so that you only appear in position 3 (the top of your range).

Takeaways:

Position Preferencing can be a powerful tool in maintaining the balance between clicks and conversions, as long as your maximum bids are high enough so that your ads continue to show.

#78 Reporting: Marketing Gold Dust

The search engines provide multiple reports to help you get the most from your campaign. For AdWords advertisers they include:

- **Keyword Performance:** Shows performance of individual keywords in detail.

- **Ad Performance:** Shows how each different ad creative has performed. Will also break out details on image and video ads.

- **Ad Group Performance:** Aggregate statistics for each ad group within your campaign.

- **URL Performance:** Gives performance statistics for each of your destination URLs.

- **Campaign Performance:** Gives top line statistics for each campaign within your account.

- **Account Performance:** An overall performance report for your account giving a snapshot at a point in time.

- **Reach and Frequency Performance:** Gives detail on the reach (how many people saw) and frequency (how often people saw) of your ads over time.

- **Search Query Performance:** Key report that shows the specific search queries that resulted in one of your ads being shown.

- **Placement Performance:** Gives a breakdown of the performance of specific content network placements.

Yahoo! and Microsoft also offer similar reporting tools within their interfaces, as do most of the second-tier networks. Don't ignore these reports as this data is marketing gold dust.

If you don't have the resources to run and digest regular reports, then it may be time to find an agency to do this work for you.

Takeaways:

The reports provided by the search engines give you the opportunity to quantify the performance of ads, keywords and targeting methods. Don't waste it.

ClickThrough
the search conversion experts

#79 Accurately Tracking Your Ads

Every major search engine has comprehensive tracking technology built into its systems. Much of the information gleaned from this tracking is available in the reports that the search engines provide to advertisers.

However, search engines do not share all the information they have about your campaign with you, which is where a third-party tracking system can help.

Many bid management systems will pass visitors through their own servers before they are sent to your website. Thanks to the speed of today's internet, this change is imperceptible to the user. The information collected can provide more detailed reports, and create a detailed history of changes to your account.

Some ad tracking tools can also give more insight on suspected click fraud; information that can help support any claim for a refund from the search engines.

Takeaways:

The use of additional tracking tools can help you to unlock additional data about your campaign.

#80 Complete The Picture With Web Analytics

The advertising reports provided by the search engines concern themselves solely with your PPC campaign. To find out what happens once someone lands on your site you need a web analytics package.

This program can help you spot trends, track user journeys throughout your site and identify new keyword terms to add to your campaign.

PPC can deliver a large number of visitors to your site but you will need a web analytics package to evaluate the quality of the traffic it provides. By following your web statistics through to sales and conversions you will be better placed to make key decisions about your campaign. Realising that good data and good decisions go hand in hand, the two largest search engines have launched their own analytics tools (google.com/analytics and web.analytics.yahoo.com) which can be integrated with your PPC accounts for greater transparency.

Takeaways:

The more you learn from your web analytics about your campaigns, the better informed your decisions will be.

Getting Your Ads In Front Of A Wider Audience

#81 Migrating To Yahoo!
And Microsoft adCenter

The most important component of any Pay Per Click campaign is Google AdWords. The wealth of targeting options, research tools and 90% global market share means that some PPC marketers refuse to spend anywhere else. However, Yahoo! and Microsoft adCenter both offer alternatives for search marketers looking to reach the largest possible audience.

Although there is plenty to recommend both Yahoo! and Microsoft, here are some of their key standout features:

Yahoo! - provides detailed reports on how the sites within their content network are performing, have intuitive scheduling features and have their own desktop account management application. Yahoo! are also able to import your AdWords account, and have a tool to convert search ads into mobile placements. Yahoo! search also has some interesting features that some searchers find appealing, such as their Search Pad research tool and query assistance.

Microsoft - offers demographic targeting, have followed Google in producing an ad preview tool that lets you check your ads are running without affecting your CTR, offer a powerful keyword research and pricing application that integrates with Excel and, crucially, Bing (Microsoft's search engine) powers the search functionality within Facebook.

However, things are set to change. In an effort to increase competition, Microsoft and Yahoo! have announced a tie-up in which Bing will power the search results, and Yahoo! provide the sales force, for both companies. This will produce a single point of contact for advertisers, with a combined global market share of almost 8%.

Takeaways:

Yahoo! and Microsoft offer alternative sources of traffic, with lower bid costs. Their new partnership will make it harder for you to avoid placing them on your ad schedule.

ClickThrough
the search conversion experts

#82 Contextual Advertising And Content Networks

The average internet user only spends one-third of their time online on sites belonging to the top ten brands (e.g. google.com, yahoo.com, facebook.com, myspace,com, apple.com, youtube.com, wikipedia.org**). The remaining two-thirds of that time is spent on small to medium size websites, forums, portals and blogs. These sites provide micro-targeted content that caters for specific hobbies and interests.**

In the past, webmasters frequently found that turning a profit from their sites took a back seat. The search engines realised that they could adapt their search technology to serve highly-targeted advertising on these sites, sharing the revenue with the website owners.

The first major program to launch was Google's AdSense program in 2003. Google reads the content of a given web-page and identifies the major keywords and themes. This data is used to find relevant ads, which are then served on the page. In 2005 Yahoo! announced the Yahoo! Publisher Network (their own version of AdSense) and Microsoft has also developed a similar product.

 ## Reach Buyers Earlier With The Content Network

The Google content network can reach people as they consume content online. Here are things to consider when creating a content network campaign:

- People exposed to content network ads may be at an earlier stage of the buying process than searchers, who already have a strong idea of what they want. You should take this into account when creating content network ads.

- The CTR on content network ads is usually far lower than standard search listings. Although this means fewer visitors, in theory you could benefit from a huge amount of low-cost advertising on sites that are relevant to your business. However, as many competing advertisers bid on a CPM basis when using the content network, this free ride is tough to achieve in practice.

- Google knows that even when people don't click on their AdSense ad units, the websites URL may be remembered and visited directly at a later date. Google now gives view-through conversion tracking, which details the number of conversions that happened within 30 days of a user seeing, but not clicking on, a content network ad. With this information you can pinpoint the sites that have the most influence on your online conversions, regardless of clicks.

- Taking a top spot on the content network is often much cheaper than on the paid SERPs. Most ad units have room for 2-3 ads, so if you can afford to maintain a high position your ad will be only one of a handful on that page.

#84 Planning Your Way To Success

Content targeting can be a very efficient way of directing ads at the right audience. For years, media agencies have used tools and consumer insight to reach tightly-defined audiences through different media channels.

Now, anyone can use DoubleClick Ad Planner (**google.com/adplanner**), free tools such as **alexa.com**, or paid tools such as **hitwise.co.uk** and try their hand at media planning.

DoubleClick Ad Planner can help you identify websites that your audience is likely to visit, using filters for age, location, gender, education and household income. You can also use keywords to find sites and subject matter categories. Once you have identified the sites of interest, you can import these into your AdWords account in order to create ads specifically to appear on these sites.

Use of these tools can help you increase the reach (number of people who see your ad) and frequency (how many times they see your ad) of your campaign. For example, IT equipment manufacturers advertise on general technology and gadget sites because they know they are visited by IT professionals in their leisure time.

#85 Cherry Picking Sites

Although poorly performing publisher sites are periodically removed from the content network, there may still be some sites on which you would prefer your ads didn't run.

Fortunately, Google allow you to block up to 5,000 sites from running your ads at a campaign level. This can stop your ads appearing on sites with an audience that is different from your target market (e.g. stopping your paid-for software ads appearing on a fiercely open source website).

Setting up site exclusion for content network campaigns can take time, but it is time well invested if it means your ad budget is directed towards the sites that will deliver the best chance of a conversion.

#86 Breaking Out Of the Text Format

The first graphical banner ad (also known as 'display' ads), promoting AT&T, appeared in 1996. Now, almost 15 years later, search engines are offering paid search marketers the opportunity to create do-it-yourself display ads using a self-service interface.

Both Google (google.com/adwords/displayadbuilder) and Yahoo! (yahoomydisplayads.adready.com) offer display ad builders, which provide tools to create both simple image ads, as well as flash and video adverts, known as 'rich media'.

Once created, the ads can be targeted to appear on sites with content that is relevant to your product or audience. Yahoo!'s service offers predefined ad templates complete with guide clickthrough rates (CTRs) based on the performance of the template enjoyed by previous advertisers.

Takeaways:
Display ads can offer you an additional route to market, and allow you to apply search marketing copy-writing expertise to a graphical format.

the search conversion experts

#87 Second Tier PPC Networks

Once you have mastered AdWords, and rolled out your campaign successfully to Yahoo! and Microsoft adCenter, you may want to try alternative PPC traffic sources.

Many of these second-tier PPC text ad networks (leaving Google, Yahoo! and Microsoft as the first-tier, premium networks) exist primarily to serve the needs of US advertisers, but a number will accept business from the UK. These networks have to work harder to offer advertisers something different:

- **7search.com**, at the time of writing, accepts bids as low as $0.01 USD per click.

- **Looksmart.com** can optimise multiple ad creatives based on a target CPA.

- **Search123.uk.com** can show your ads on a number of shopping comparison sites in the UK.

- **AdKnowledge.com** can show your ad on social networks, currently serving over ten billion ad impressions a month on these sites.

- **Adbrite.com** is able to target by gender, age and country. They also offer fullpage ads, which appear when a visitor first lands on a page in their network.

- **Bidvertiser.com** allows those websites which show their ads to create customised ad sizes, which can mean your ads can appear in places that other networks can't reach.

Other networks to consider include **abcsearch.com**, **marchex.com**, **findology.com** and **chitika.com**, although there are many more.

You should start with a small budget on these networks, as traffic quality can vary.

However, these networks can help bring down your average cost per click.

#88 Social Network Ads

By far the biggest change in online behaviour in recent years has been the rise in social network usage. Social networks dominate the time spent online for large numbers of people today.

Here's how the major social networks are using PPC to fund their services:

- Facebook (facebook.com/advertising) allows you to target your text ad according to gender, relationship status, location, workplace and education. Onpage keywords can also be used to trigger ads. If a user indicates that they like a particular ad, this is then shown to their friends also.

- MySpace (advertise.myspace.com) have their own display ad builder, and add in the ability to target by parental status (e.g with kids, no kids, expecting) and interests.

- Business network LinkedIn (linkedin.com/directads) provide a link at the bottom of their text ads straight back to the person who created them, which can boost credibility. You can choose the type of person to whom your ad will be shown based on their job function, company size, sector and even seniority.

#89 Using Twitter Ad Networks To Broaden Your Reach

Twitter has exploded in popularity in recent years. According to Google Trends, twitter.com now has more daily worldwide traffic than microsoft.com and bing.com combined at the time of writing.

Twitter has announced that it will offer pay per click advertising within their onsite search results to monetise its service. Nevertheless, a number of third-party ad networks have sprung up to provide marketers with a way of distributing their text ads using widely read Twitter accounts.

Networks such as twittad.com, betweeted.com, ad.ly, adcause.com, tweetroi.com and sponsoredtweets.com aggregate Twitter users who tweet about an advertiser's product or service in exchange for a fee. As the search engines are now including feeds from social networks such as Twitter towards the top of their natural search results, these ad networks can give you extra search engine coverage at a relatively low price.

#90 Video Ads And PPC

Google, Yahoo! and Microsoft all offer video search products, and are keen to monetise what can be an expensive service to provide.

AdWords advertisers may already be appearing within video content, as their contextually-targeted text ads can be overlaid over the bottom of Google-owned YouTube videos.

However, Google content network advertisers with existing video ad content can also use pay per click pricing as opposed to paying each time their video is played. Yahoo! has also been incorporating video ads directly in PPC text ad placements through their "Rich Ads in Search" program.

ClickThrough
the search conversion experts

#91 The Rise Of Personalised Ads

Behavioural targeting is a technology which allows for personalisation of the ads shown to a consumer, based on depersonalised past data about the sites they visited, the searches they made, and the ads they interacted with.

Google has now introduced this type of advertising with their opt-out 'interest-based advertising' product within AdSense. Yahoo! has also launched the opt-in 'Consumer Connect' scheme in the UK, using loyalty card data to serve display ads based on past purchasing decisions.

For example, some user searches may not trigger any ads, as the keywords used are not being bid on by an advertiser. Behavioural targeting would enable the search engines to mine recent search activity for that user, and then serve alternative ads based on a previous search, rather than the present one. This technique is already being used within the AdSense network, serving ads on one website, based on the subject of another website that the user may have visited hours before.

Takeaways:
Despite privacy concerns, behavioural targeting will be a key part of the development of online advertising in future.

What's Next In PPC?

#92 The Ad Next Door - PPC Goes Local

Many companies will always be local in outlook e.g. funeral directors, dry cleaners. Fortunately, the emergence of local pay per click services means that these businesses can now advertise effectively online.

To create a local PPC campaign, consider the different geographic and regional terms which are relevant to your business. These could be town names, county, neighbouring areas, even country names (e.g. Wales, Scotland). Microsoft provide a tool (adlab.msn.com/Location-Platform) which can help you expand a local keyword list.

The addition of a geographical term to a keyword could help bring click costs down and relevancy up.

Local businesses can now benefit from "Location" ads. These placements build on existing local search

campaigns, but build in additional information that help confirm supplier suitability in the consumer's mind. This could include a postal address, a phone number, the location of the store on a Google Map and a link to directions, all from within the ad.

This is another powerful example of organic and paid search techniques working together, and a reminder of the importance of adding every branch of your business to maps.google.com, bing.com/maps and local.yahoo.com.

#93

Mobile Pay Per Click - Ads On the Move

The growing popularity of smart phones means that millions of people are now browsing on the move.

The incorporation of GPS technology into mobile phones means that search engines can provide even users who don't know their exact location with relevant answers, and of course, locally targeted ads.

Google, Yahoo! and Microsoft all offer mobile PPC products, and even allow you to target consumers based on the operating system of their phone (e.g. iPhone or Google Android-based phones). Google has also recently introduced 'pay per call' ads, charging advertisers when a number is highlighted and called from a mobile ad viewed by a smartphone user.

Mobile ads pose a new challenge to search marketers. Google mobile ads only allow for 36 characters (18 characters each for the headline and body text) so ads need to have a single, strong call to action.

 #94

Form Extensions: The Reward For Being In Top Position

Google has recently added the ability to incorporate a contact form into your paid search ad, giving you the option to gather leads from a drop down option within your ad itself, rather than from a form on your site.

Your prospect will be asked for their name, contact number and address, plus up to three additional questions. Any leads delivered to an advertiser during this beta (experimental) test will be charged at their maximum cost per click. Advertisers are also required to follow up prospects' calls within 24 hours.

From early 2010 form extensions are only available to advertisers in the top position for a keyword and who have a US phone number, but it is likely that this will be rolled out internationally once beta testing has been concluded.

Takeaways:

The recent purchase of mobile ad networks by Google and Apple indicates that mobile advertising will be a major focus from now on.

ClickThrough
the search conversion experts

#95 Prepare To Be Compared

The recent global recession has taken online comparison shopping to new levels of popularity. The search engines, ever keen to take advantage of consumer demand, have moved to strengthen their own comparison offerings.

In late 2009 Google announced that it would be offering a Pay Per Lead comparison engine to help users review financial products in a single page of results. Once a user has decided which products or services, offers or deals are of most interest to them, there is an option either to call a number requesting further information or request a quotation.

The potential customer's privacy is protected by directing the enquiry through Google rather than directly to the supplier.

The downside to this model is that some websites may not have the resources to cope with a large number of enquiries. To counteract this, it is possible that this will become an opt-in rather than opt-out model.

#96 Sitelinks - Another Bite Of The Cherry

Organic listings on Google have long included up to eight additional 'site links' (additional links to specific areas of your website) to assist users.

Site link functionality is now available to PPC advertisers, with up to four site links appearing underneath some ads.

However, site links are not available to all advertisers, as Google decides whether your ads are eligible using their own quality guidelines.

You can discover whether you are eligible for PPC site links within your AdWords account. Choose a Campaign, then select 'Settings', and scroll down to 'Networks, Extensions and Devices'. If the 'Ad Extensions' category is available then this is proof of eligiblity.

Add a tracker URL for the sitelink itself so that you can judge whether or not they are working for you and not distracting visitors from high yield pages e.g. 'http://www.your-companys-site.com/contactus.asp?sitelink'.

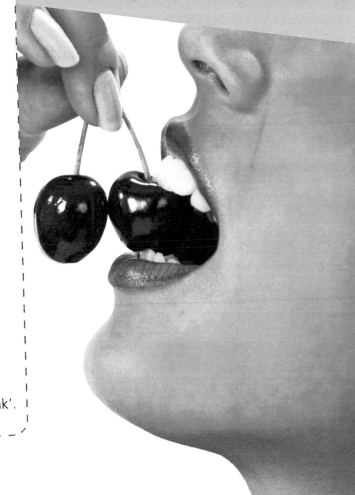

One of the benefits of linking your different Google accounts is that different Google products are then able to work together.

That has always been true for AdWords and Analytics, but is now also true for your Merchant Centre Account. If your ad has been triggered by a search term, Google can now check to see if you have any products listed in your Merchant Centre Account that are also relevant to the search. If you have, these are automatically appended to the bottom of your ad, including any product images, names and prices you have uploaded.

Simply link your Merchant Centre Account to your AdWords account by entering your AdWords ID in your Merchant Centre Account.

To add your products within a campaign, you need to go to Networks, Extensions and Devices under Settings for that campaign, and edit your ad extensions. There are optional parameters that can also be set up, which are similar to exact match and broad match, as well as offering tracking and redirects for special offers.

#98 Multi-Lingual PPC Campaigns

As business becomes more global in outlook, multi-lingual PPC campaigns are becoming more commonplace. However, they aren't for the faint-hearted.

Here are some potential pitfalls:

• Most translators produce precise, literal translations of documents. However, the language used by consumers when searching online can be very colloquial, and search volume of a phrase matters far more to a search marketer than whether it is grammatically correct.

• PPC campaigns need to be built to best fit the market for which they are destined. The structure of ad groups is usually derived from the keywords within them, and so you need to treat each country as a new account. If you run your account in five countries, expect your workload to increase five-fold!

• Each market has different advertising rules and regulations that need to be adhered to. This is one of the benefits of working with an agency who has prior experience in your territories.

Takeaways:

Multi-market PPC campaigns can be very intensive, and if they go wrong there can be serious consequences. It may be worth using an agency to manage this process for you.

the search conversion experts

#99 Being Timely; Exploiting Events As They Happen

It only takes minutes to create a PPC ad, which allows you to react very quickly to a breaking news story or a sudden surge in interest for a product or service within your sector.

Running ads in response to real time news and events can often bring you shortlived but effective advertising opportunities.

By setting up Twitter and Google alerts you can quickly find if there are any breaking news stories triggered by your keywords.

You can also use Dynamic Keyword Insertion **(#35)** so that you have ads which are shown as soon as searches for a specific term take off.

#100 Why You Need An Agency

Many companies find that they don't have the time or resource to commit to managing a large PPC campaign, day in, day out. They prefer to outsource to experts, who have experience in running profitable PPC campaigns across multiple sectors, rather than employ costly specialist staff in-house.

The process of choosing an agency can be daunting, with a number of agencies claiming to provide the best service. If you are thinking of working with an agency, or looking to move your existing account, here's what to look for:

• A good agency will take time to evaluate your overall business goals, and create a bespoke strategy that meets your needs, rather than push you toward an out-of-the-box solution.

• Better agencies will have a formalised training programme in place, and will encourage their staff to attain industry accreditations, such as the AdWords Professional qualification.

• A reputable agency will offer a no-obligation review of your account. That way, you will be able to understand exactly how they intend to improve things before you choose to work with them.

• To ensure business continuity your agency should also provide you with access to a full account management team. This will also ensure that you have a senior member of staff to turn to should any issues arise.

• A quality agency will permit you full ownership of your own data.

• Avoid agencies that try to force you into a long term contract.

Continuing Your PPC Journey

Your PPC campaign should evolve over time, but remember that everything you do should add value to your bottom line. It can be too easy to think that just because a specific keyword is driving a large number of visitors to your site, it is generating money for you. It is only by looking more deeply into your stats that you will get the full picture of a keyword's effectiveness.

Whilst this analysis may take time, it will pay back in spades if you can identify the keywords that not only bring in visitors, but also produce sales and conversions.

Set measurable goals so that you are able to drill down into each keyword or ad's performance and observe the typical user journey through the site for each. Monitor the number of calls, email enquiries and sales generated from each visit to your site and calculate what each activity is worth to you.

Finally, **ClickThrough-Marketing.com** has produced a range of up-to-date guides to help you on your internet marketing journey, so check out our site.

ClickThrough
the search conversion experts